The Connection Between the Absolute and the Relative

A Conversation with Shaykh Fadhlalla Haeri

Shaykh Fadhlalla Haeri

Publisher: Zahra Publications

http://www.zahrapublications.pub

Published in June of 2019

ISBN (E-Book): NONE

ISBN (Paperback): 978-1-928329-12-1

Cover Photo: Rasooli Center Mosque Dome, Pretoria, South Africa.

Cover Design and Photo Taken by Anjum Jaleel.

Table of Contents

Publisher's Note

This conversation between the late John Giancarlo and Shaykh Fadhlalla Haeri took place in 1990 and was televised on TV ISLAM INTERNATIONAL in Ontario, Canada in 1992.

In it, Shaykh Fadhlalla talks about wide-ranging topics, which are as relevant today as they were when this conversation was first held, for it presents Islam as the archetypal, universal, Adamic path that began when humanity rose in consciousness to recognize duality and began its journey from the relative back to Absolute Unity.

We recently published it as an eBook,[1] and are now publishing it as a paperback book, with slight editing.

---

[1] At the end of this book, is a complete list of eBooks we have published.

About Shaykh Fadhlalla Haeri

Acknowledged as a master of self-knowledge and a spiritual philosopher, Shaykh Fadhlalla Haeri's role as a teacher grew naturally out of his own quest for self-fulfillment.

He travelled extensively on a spiritual quest which led to his eventual rediscovery of the pure and original Islamic heritage of his birth, and the discovery of the truth that reconciles the past with the present, the East with the West, the worldly with the spiritual – a link between the ancient wisdom teachings and our present time.

A descendant of five generations of well-known and revered spiritual leaders, Shaykh Fadhlalla Haeri has taught students throughout the world for over 30 years. A prolific author of more than thirty books relating to the universal principles of Islam, the Qur'an, and its core purpose of enlightenment, he is a gifted exponent of how the self relates to the soul, humankind's link with the Divine, and how consciousness can be groomed to reflect our higher nature.

The unifying scope of his perspective emphasizes practical, actionable knowledge that leads to self-transformation, and provides a natural bridge between seemingly different Eastern and Western approaches to spirituality, as well as offering a common ground of higher knowledge for various religions, sects and secular outlooks.

About John Giancarlo

John Giancarlo, who passed away in 2018 at the age of 90, was an educator in Canada. He began his teaching career in Niagara with the Crowland Public School system in 1949.

In 1956 he was appointed Principal of Maple Leaf School in Welland, and continued his career as a Principal until 1967, when he accepted a position as the Chairman of Humanities at the newly constructed Niagara College, and went on to become Dean of Applied Arts as the College grew and developed.

His great curiosity about our world and the universe led him to enjoy reading books on many topics including science, philosophy, nature, health and medicine. He had a keen interest in other people and showed great thoughtfulness and generosity.

Introduction *by* **John Giancarlo**

This interview was conducted with the hope that it would help people to better understand the concepts of Islam and to lead them to a higher level of reverence for God and greater level of spiritual fulfillment. Islam signifies submission to God, and a Muslim is one who submits to God. Muslims, Christians and Jews are united by their belief in One Divine Being, variously named God, Jehovah or Allah, who enjoins us to respect life and to love one another. They also share the belief of the survival of the inner self or soul after the body dies.

Unfortunately, the popular media often report the tragic occurrences that tend to cause division among people of different religions, cultures and races, rather than those events which unite us. In this booklet, Shaykh Fadhlalla Haeri discusses the ideals and practices that, if followed, can enrich and unite all humanity. It was my good fortune to meet Shaykh Fadhlalla, to question him and hear the inspirational message that he delivered during my interview with him.

The initial meeting was arranged by Tayie Rahem, the producer of TV ISLAM INTERNATIONAL. On a rainy morning in May of 1990, I received a telephone call from Tayie to advise me that Shaykh Fadhlalla was visiting in the area, and asked me if I could meet with them.

As Director of Umma Television Productions based in St. Catherines, Ontario, Tayie wished to film my interview with television across Canada. Tayie and I had just returned from a trip to Italy and Spain where we had filmed a series of television documentaries on Islam in Rome and Granada. In Italy, we were invited by the Director of the Islamic Cultural Center in Rome, Abdul-Qayuum Khan, to visit the new mosque under construction just about 3 miles from the Vatican. An indication of the positive changes that are occurring among religious groups is that the Vatican now has an official representative, whose role it is to serve as the liaison official of the Catholic Church with the Muslim community. Our interview with Father Michel at the Vatican revealed the sympathetic attitude of the Church that now exists towards people of other faiths and Muslims in particular.

As we travelled through countries of Europe by train, Tayie and I had a great deal of time to discuss such matters as religion, values, morality, ethics, the self, and many of the ideas that Shaykh Fadhlalla had written about in his book, *The Journey of the Self*. I had received a copy of this book almost a year before our trip to Europe and had read the book a number of times. It took me some time to get used to the style of writing, terminology and the original ideas it contained.

When Shaykh Fadhlalla talks about the heart being "empty", for example, he does not mean it is devoid of feeling; rather, he refers to one's heart being free of the anger, hatred, greed, or envy, that in actuality interferes with the bliss a person is capable of experiencing. The underlying theme of the book is the development of one's inner-self, right action in this life and the unity of the self with the Infinite.

As we drove to meet Shaykh Fadhlalla in St. Catharines, I jotted down a few questions I wanted to ask him about the thoughts he had expressed in his book on the self. Shaykh Fadhlalla greeted us with very warm welcome. The peace and joy that he radiated put us immediately at ease and the conversation flowed freely between us. As a Sufi teacher, Shaykh Fadhlalla has many followers and has written extensively on the subject of Sufism in his book, *The Elements of Sufism*. There is some speculation on the origin of the word *sufi*, but according to some authorities the term is derived from the Arabic word '*safa*', which means purity. A Sufi is a person who seeks the path of inner enlightenment and purification of the heart. Sufism is "the heart of Islam" according to Shaykh Fadhlalla, and its followers aim at the improvement of their character and behavior as part of their submission to God. Spiritual progress is achieved by abandoning attachments to the material world, and pursuing the awakening of the inner life as a necessary condition to achieving fulfillment as a human being. Shaykh Fadhlalla writes that, "The true art of Sufism leads towards the steady state of being contented, integrated, wise, courteous, kind and at peace". These are the very qualities that I observed Shaykh Fadhlalla to have during our meeting that day in May. It was these admirable qualities that he himself had achieved that drew me to a contemplation of his message.

The taping of my interview took place at Niagara-on-the-Lake at the home of Dr. Sahin, an eminent physician, and a major supporter of TV ISLAM. Tayie Rehem filmed almost continuously for about 4 hours, stopping only to reload the camera periodically.

No part of the interview was rehearsed. Shaykh Fadhlalla spoke completely extemporaneously and with great enthusiasm. Some of the questions I addressed to him were those that I had planned to ask, but as Shaykh Fadhlalla spoke most of my comments and questions arose spontaneously. The result was a message that came completely from the heart as sincere and inspirational as one could ever wish to hear.

When Tayie produced the tapes to be aired on national television during the month of Ramadan in 1991, I was amazed as I heard once again the voice of Shaykh Fadhlalla. His words had an even greater impact as I heard them again. It occurred to me that the tapes should be transcribed and made available in a booklet for convenience and easy reference so that one might read and reflect on the words of this renowned spiritual teacher. The idea received the unqualified support of Shaykh Fadhlalla and his friends.

Ultimately, a Sufi teacher has written, "enlightenment is a gift from Allah". We can compare ignorance to darkness and knowledge to light or enlightenment. In the translation of the Qur'an by Abdullah Yusuf Ali we find the following commentary on Light: "So men of God who preach God's truth are themselves illuminated by God's Light and become the illuminating media through which that Light spreads and permeates human life". Shaykh Fadhlalla is a Sufi teacher who has been given the gift of enlightenment, and in turn strives to illuminate the path for others.

Introduction *by* John Giancarlo

Love and Peace[2] were chosen as part of the title because of their prominence in Shaykh Fadhlalla's thoughts. He has written, "It is by love that we are propelled towards contentment and fulfillment". Love takes many forms but the most satisfying is the love of God. It is through this love that we achieve peace.

One of the divine names of God is "As-Salaam", or Peace. The achievement of true peace within ourselves is accompanied by a great joy and a love for all creation. The other equally important aspect of love is the love of humankind and indeed for all that God has created. It is written in the Qur'an that, *"Everyone in heaven and earth entreats Him; every day He is at work."*[3]

In this passage we observe the word 'shine' which denotes God's light. God is ever merciful and compassionate. Shaykh Fadhlalla notes that another of the divine names of God is *"Al-Jamal"*, the Beautiful. A prophetic Muslim proverb states: "Allah is beautiful and

---

[2] **Publisher's Note:** At Shaykh Fadhlalla's suggestion, it is being published under the title, *The Connection Between the Absolute and the Relative.*

[3] Qur'an 55:29

loves beauty". Shaykh Fadhlalla is also realistic in acknowledging that the world, though beautiful, is beset by problems, tragedy, and strife. There is among its people competition for, as well as waste of, food, water, and natural resources. Poverty, ignorance and many evils abound. These problems, however, cannot be laid at the doorstep of God. They are the inevitable results of man's inaction and unwillingness to work together with others in solving human problems. Shaykh Fadhlalla writes, "As long as there is injustice there will be agitation and turmoil preventing the possibility of lasting peace". It behooves us, all enlightened persons of all faiths, therefore, to do all within our power to help in eliminating prejudice, hate, and injustice and promoting understanding, brotherhood, and peace. Such is the aim of Shaykh Fadhlalla as his words and actions testify. In the words of the Qur'an: *"But as for those who believe and do good deeds, their Lord will guide them because of their faith. Streams will flow at their feet in the Gardens of Bliss. Their prayer in them will be, 'Glory be to You,*

God!' their greeting, 'Peace,' and the last part of their prayer, 'Praise be to God, Lord of the Worlds.'"[4]

May the words of Shaykh Fadhlalla in this booklet bring light to your life, love to your heart and peace to your soul.

John Giancarlo, January 22, 1992

---

[4] Qur'an 10:9-10

The Meaning of Islam and Muslims

Q: I wonder if you could begin by giving us the definition of the words "Islam" and "Muslim", for those of us who do not know the meaning of these words?

The Arabic language is one of those unusual languages that can communicate things that are not easily communicable. It is not unlike Aramaic or Sanskrit, and the roots of most terms are made up of three letter clusters. Whoever takes up Arabic for spiritual awakening or enlightenment, or for the unfathomable in the Qur'an, will find an incredible delight in its discovery. The word *islam* usually is thought to have originated from the three letters: "*sīn, lām, mīm*", from "*salama*"; which means *to be at peace, to be saved, to be wholesome, to be in a state of tranquil submission – acceptable submissiveness*. It is the path of ease and of integration; it is the path of submission to reality because we are part of that reality, we are not separate from it. It is the way from time immemorial; it is not something that occurred some 1400

1

years ago. It is the "*dīn*", it is the only way to be, which has been expounded by every prophet, messenger and sage. It is how to integrate into physical beingness, visible beingness, with the invisible, because we have emanated from it. It means to know in order to unify with the occurrence as we experience it and as we interact with it.

The outer courtesy of it is to have every creation safe for Muslims who practice Islam, to interact with the rest of creation courteously, harmoniously, joyfully, correctly, with barriers, not accepting transgression. It is not that everything is all right outwardly; everything is not all right outwardly: if I transgress, there must be containment and those containments are only in order to have nature and natural situations to take care of themselves, for us not to transgress.

One Unitive Source

Q: You speak of the law of opposites and complementarity. Would you elaborate on this law?

It is basically based on faith and trust, that there is one source, one essence from which every visible and invisible creation has emanated – one essence, which is beyond time and space, which encompasses experiential time and space, from that unitive source, which is God, which is the divine essence, Allah.

This passage in time and the realization of the other dimensions, such as space, begin to occur and in it all creational, visible and invisible realities have come about. They are all encompassed in that unitive totality. It is for this reason that we, even in our day-to-day existential experiences, want to relate, interact, connect, and understand.

Understanding is in fact a manifestation of the adoration of the unitive factor. We want to inter-link. The fact that we do not understand is a deterrent; it is

3

something we do not like, which means that what we like is that which connects, understands, knows and relates. We do not like disconnection, we like connection, and this is a proof of that unitive force at play at all times.

Unity & Duality

Q: Regardless of our differences of religion, nationality, race, political beliefs, as people, we have derived from one source and that there should be a link and goodwill among human beings. What are your views on this matter?

If there is any deprivation or any negligence of that unitive awakening, it is because of our own lack of evolvement. In life we experience every physical or sensual situation as one of two. Anything that manifests, or has come about, been born or brought about, created in time and space, is one of two forces. There is always duality: man/woman, day/ night, good/bad, healthy/unhealthy, breathing in/breathing out, sleep/awake, generous/mean, whether it is values or physical matters, such as hard/soft, and so on. Whatever manifests itself is one of two opposites, and we constantly seek a balance, constantly seek to be in the middle, whether it is in health or wealth. We constantly want to be

5

in equilibrium. Therefore, outwardly there is a struggle, which is unavoidable, and yet inwardly we seek peace, tranquility, calmness, love, serenity, and centrality – what we call "beingness". We all, as human beings, are inadvertently caught in what appears to be a contradiction: outwardly, we are subjected to these opposites; and yet, inwardly, we seek a state that transcends these opposites.

In your question, you say there are differences in religions: there are no differences if they have emanated from the same source. If they are pseudo-religions or human-made religions or human-made laws, then it is something else.

If they have emanated from that same original unitive source, then there are no differences in religions. There can be differences between religiosity and religious people, but it is us who have created them, either because of cultural, historical or linguistic differences.

As you know, even now, if what we are speaking about is translated or related by a third party it is bound to be, even with the best of will, somewhat changed – not necessarily completely distorted, but relayed with different emphasis, especially if that third party comes from a different culture and language, from a language that was not a prophetically revealed one and therefore not a *transmittive* teaching.

Differences were to do with the presence of that prophetic being; they were not factually, describable, physical events, they were transformative realities. A being like the Prophet Muhammad (Peace be upon him), whose heart was beyond time and space and who functioned amongst people, to help them evolve to that inner reality is not something you and I can imbibe from a book or from a film made on him.

God, Prophets and Religion

Q: Shaykh Fadhlalla, you brought up a very interesting point, that there is only one God, and therefore, only one religion and the praise of that one God, and yet, we find religions such as Judaism, Christianity, Buddhism, Islam – these are major world religions. Why would God reveal these various religions? And how can a person choose among them?

There are no various religions. They are manifestations from the same source, they are revealed knowledges by these incredible beings, these 'transformers of man' called prophets and messengers. And incidentally, in Islam we are told that there were 124,000 of them, so we believe that there have been on occasions hundreds and hundreds of messengers in one locality. It is these beings who awaken to the inner reality that there is one source that has created all this, and that everything is returning to that source and is sustained by that one source, and the purpose of creation is none other than to adore, or worship, or to know that source, which is based on love and abandonment into it. Each and every culture, tribe and civilization had access to this sort of event.

Most of these civilizations and cultures had a prophet or a messenger or an awakened being. Now the differences are amongst the people, amongst the interpretations. There would be no differences between these prophets; they would all be together having a wonderful time and acknowledging the one source that they were plugged into within themselves, but it were the people around them who would create the misinterpretations. It is because of the club syndrome and the insecurity of human beings that we feel more secure with a certain backdrop, language, culture, diet or whatever.

The Qur'an

Q: You mentioned that there are certain Arabic words that convey meaning that is difficult to convey when it is translated into another language. Professor (Ibrahim) Stokes, one of your students, mentioned that he was studying Arabic so that he could appreciate the Qur'an better. I have read a translation of the Qur'an. Can the person who reads the Qur'an in translation really get as much out of it, or do you have to read it in the original?

There are, of course, degrees of how much we can get out of the Qur'an. The Qur'an is the book of knowledge, and the book of knowledge essentially also exists in the heart of the seeker of knowledge. The other side of the coin, the microcosmic aspect of the Qur'an, is in the human heart. Allah says, *"The heavens and the earth do not contain me, but the heart of he who has faith in me contains me."* The Qur'an is Allah's word, so potentially we contain it, but the extent of that unveiling is dependent upon the extent of our ability to have that pure approach and the linguistic openings, so to speak.

There are various degrees of good and bad translations, but if one wants to really see the mosaic, the *transmittiveness* of the terms and of some of the sentences, then we have to go to the Arabic of that time, not necessarily the Arabic that is spoken nowadays. A lot of the terms that are in the Qur'an are now found in ordinary Arabic language but they are distorted; they do not mean exactly the same thing. In order to have that infinite vista we must go to the original Arabic, and it is not that difficult. It is not a difficult language, if one approaches it from this angle.

Allah

Q: One of the great sayings that has impressed upon me, is from the Qur'an, wherein Allah says, "We are closer to him than his jugular vein"[5] Does that mean that Allah is always with us?

In fact, Islam is founded on the proclamation that there is no reality except Allah. There is no possibility except by Allah and from Allah and unto Allah. It says in the Qur'an: *"Wherever you turn is the face of Allah."*[6] Whatever has manifested has occurred from Allah. Abandonment of other than Allah is submission; that is, *being in Islam*. It is the realization that there cannot be *otherness*; the *otherness* is only shadow-play of the oneness that encompasses this apparent dual otherness.

So: where is it that Allah is not? Elsewhere in the Qur'an it says: *"Oh man, you are striving and no matter what you are striving for, it is in the way of Allah."* But

---

[5] Qur'an 50:16

[6] Qur'an 2:115

the difference is, do I know it? Or am I clumsily just stumbling? Am I on the way consciously or am I just stumbling along in my whims and in my imagination and fantasies? This is the difference!

Oneness of Humankind

Q: As you are aware, Shaykh Fadhlalla, Jesus said that all the laws and the Prophets can be boiled down to two: To love God with your whole heart, whole soul, and to love your neighbor as yourself. Is this also a teaching in Islam?

In fact, one definition of a Muslim is that he will not sleep the night if there is one person who has not had enough supper that night in that town. He is not a Muslim if he sleeps the night in comfort knowing that there is one person anywhere within that city who has not had enough to eat. The Qur'an says: *"He who kills one person has killed the entire creation, and he who brings back to life [or enlivens or awakens or helps to bring light to the heart of] one person is as though he has brought into life the entire creation."*[7] Allah says in the Qur'an: *"I created from one self"*[8]. There is one macro-self and we are the

---

[7] Qur'an 5:32

[8] Qur'an 4:1

micro-selves. Each one of us is a microcosm: we reflect the entire cosmos. If you do not respect the image of this microcosm in your neighbor and friend then you have no respect for the source of it.

History of Islam

Q: In the early history of Islam the Muslims achieved a great civilization. What are the differences between Islam then and now? And why do Muslims worldwide suffer from a bad image today?

If you look back historically at the time of the advent of the Prophet Muhammad (Peace and Mercy be upon him) about 1400 odd years ago, there was such darkness in the world. Christianity as it was known, especially in that part of the world, in the Middle-East, had fallen into a considerable disarray and decadence, and so were most other religions in that part of the world. Also, there was no revealed Prophet to the Arabs as such, at the time of this occurrence, so this light emanating through this person was a reminder of the Creator and the reminder that man has to fulfill the purpose of creation.

Islam, in a sense, spread out so quickly, filling that void, within a matter of seventy years. If you recall history, it spread almost for a distance of more than 5000 km and it went all the way to Andalusia, or to Spain, and all the way to the East to the doors of China within a very short period of time. It was a timely factor since there was much darkness, and this effulgent light of being with God and behaving as befits a human beings filled that void and people embraced it, and were reminded of their own cultures that became decadent and so on. The Christians in North Africa, who were all Unitarians, simply found this to be the same that they believed in and that was all – there was no discord.

Islam never spread by the sword. Some kings and rulers did use the sword in order to expand territories and kingdoms, but you can not force people to have faith in a unitive oneness in which they have already emerged but yet not merged with. This was the event in early Islam; it was transformative, if you had trust in Allah, trusting that you will get what you need at the time you need it, rather than constantly speculating about the future and fearing about provisions over the unknown. There was real trust and that created, if you like, higher quality of human beingness among these people, and as a result the world also succumbed to them. But soon after that, like most cyclical events, people became more and more dependent upon the paraphernalia that physically surrounds them and the craziness of day-to-day life, so they forgot the purpose of existence is to adore and sing this eternal song that reality and it encompasses us and we are kings and kingdoms and the usual human jealousy, greed and other lower aspects of man. If we are not always careful, the lower aspects overcome the higher aspects. If we do not remind ourselves of the need for generosity and sharing, we end up being very selfish and very insular. So this is what happened over a period of five to six hundred years; after this effulgent light, you find the disarray amongst Muslim kings. Decadence and corruption began to set in, and it is from that era onward that we need to distinguish between Muslims and Islam.

Historically you can say that the first seven hundred years were the spread of this light, and the next seven hundred years it is shrinkage and being translated into a cultural or a religious way of behavior, rather than a 'deen' – the transaction between Allah, the Bestower and the indebted man. Islam is not a religion: it is a way of being. It is a debt to pay upon ourselves by ourselves to regain our higher selves.

Spiritual Revival

Q: Do you see a renaissance in Islam today? Is there a reaching out for perhaps a return to some of the great times of the religion in the past?

I can only use the foundation of Qur'an to answer that question. The Qur'an does not tell us that this way, this unitive awakening, what we call Islam, began 1400 years ago. It calls the first Adamic awakening, the prophet Adam, it calls him a Muslim. The Qur'an refers to all the prophets and messengers as being in Islam, so it is not something that began 1400 years ago. The prophet Muhammad was the last of the great prophets, the last and the seal of Prophethood. He did not invent Islam, it did not start in Arabia, it culminated in Arabia. We consider all prophets and all religions are Islamic and therefore we also believe that the need of spiritual awakening will continuously occur as long as there is humankind on this earth.

There will always be resurgence whenever there is increased materialism, decadence or other forms of oppression in life. The spirit within man will not accept it as a total way of life, and will rebel or want to have its nourishment. And spiritual nourishment is spiritual revival. The answer to your question is yes, but not in the conventional sense that the 'Muslims' will prevail, that is not the issue. The last fifty or sixty years we have given a great deal of emphasis to material well-being. And material well-being is a necessary condition, but it is not sufficient. The antidote or its equivalent is spiritual well-being. The yearning for inner awakening and inner light is certainly increasing, so there is a renaissance and awakening of Islam, no doubt about it.

Q: Shaykh Fadhlalla you speak of re-awakening of the spirit and improvement in that area, but in our society, and this is perhaps worldwide, there are many technological advances and there is growth and knowledge, yet at the same time there seems to be no corresponding growth in moral and ethical values. In fact, what I see is that there is a rise in crime and immorality and godlessness, and this seems to reflect a decline. Could you comment on that situation?

I am sure you are right. It is also becoming universal, because the world is so much closer nowadays than it was in the past. I consider these times as the darkness of the night before dawn. I think we have given excessive attention to the outer technological advancement and outer emancipation from the physical limitations, and we have not given enough attention to the inner potentialities and the inner qualities within man.

We have basically created a situation in our civilizations, nowadays, of total discontent: the individual is discontent, the family is discontent, the society is discontent, the nation and the world is discontent. That has a lot to do with consumption, consumerism, excess and this headlong, competitive, aggressive way to acquisition of the outer.

We have been, so to speak, wrongly educated and diverted from the balanced way. We all are subjected to physical limitations, we need to be fed, clothed and sheltered, but we have made that as our ultimate objective rather than inner fulfillment and inner awakening. That is why we all now have to be entertained.

Horizontally we are mobile; we are roaming around the world but there is no vertical mobility; we can not go inward, because in a way our inward is dark and has not been developed. We need the inward development along with the outer development, but it has gone out of balance. I trust in nature, I trust in the creator of nature, I trust in God that it will revert. But it could be after catastrophes; it may not revert in a very easy or in any smooth way, it may be after certain major jerks.

This is because we have made our god the materialistic, technological, economical monetarist growth, as though there is no end to that. Obviously the poorer are suffering more and the so-called rich countries are becoming outwardly richer but inwardly poorer. It is only that I trust in the natural balance of events in the world that I think it will revert; I do not have a great deal of outer evidence to show you. In fact, the evidences are as you say.

Finding True Happiness

Q: There seems to be a spirit of acquisition that is perhaps fostered today by the media, particularly television, where, as you have mentioned, people are becoming more and more acquisitive, and they believe that through acquiring material goods there will be happiness, and yet there is a great unhappiness. What are some of the things that people can do to achieve happiness, beyond mere acquisition of material goods?

It is a process of displacement. We all want to have pleasure, we all want to have joy, we all want to have satisfaction, but once we assume that satisfaction is based on acquiring something or is based on a desire that will be fulfilled then it is a never-ending process, because our never-ending permutations of desires and possibilities of outer acquisitions, there is no end to outer possibilities of stimulation. This is why we are, in a way, falling over ourselves with quick demands, desires and neutralization of that desire: instant gratification, because it makes us feel better, but it is only a false feeling; it is an emotion, a concept that has no reality.

Our reality is based on inner tranquility and contentment – we are by nature content. That is why we love contentment, but we have made each other discontent by agitating our minds and creating all these concepts, artificial needs and anxieties. We are running to satisfy one desire after another which are all self, society or market induced.

So, we have been caught in that artificial, false elusive illusory process that we are alive and we are living because it is all based on identifying with an outer 'thing'. We are not a 'thing', we are a being! We need certain things but we are now caught in that wheel of continuous outer entertainment and no inner attainment. No doubt, the attempt of all prophets, messengers, and all the religions converge into this very point: that through faith and trust in the unknown, in God or Allah who permeates and who engulfs the known, through that genuine, sincere trust we will come to see how our visible world is only a tiny fraction of that total invisible reality. From those few little insights and windows to the unknown we will begin to taste the art or technology of inner gratification, awareness or awakening. This is the root of gnosis. Unless we sublimate, and begin to displace the outer gratification with inner awakening we will continuously be caught in this dual, destructive and unending state of greed, acquisition and total materialistic disaster.

Q: There are spiritual teachings that say that this world is only a shadow of reality? Do you hold this belief? Will you please elaborate on it?

Reality encompasses all possible, visible, measurable, non-measurable, experienceable realities. What we are accustomed to in this body and in this world, during this short lifetime, are the realities that we interact with and interrelate to with our senses. So, there are the physical laws of nature, the interactional laws of human beings, and also my own observation of my inner self – these are realities. There is an individual situation within me and there is also a sociological inter-relationship between me and my neighbors and society. There is also the outer physical world, which we are part of, and not away from. We are part of this total, physical passage in time, caught in a biological riddle.

So this is where we are, and if we get to grips with this unitive reality then we find it is a platform from which we will occasionally be allowed to peek into the unknown, it is like being on the tip of the iceberg, the rest is submerged, but if we have not mastered the nature of what is visible and available to us it will be unnatural and not just for us to be able to see the unknown. People would dabble into magic, supernatural or try to gain power through illicit or semi-illicit means to that unknown. The natural ways for us is to master the nature of time, before we can talk about non-time. What is the nature of reality right now, before we can talk about reality beyond time and space. There is a courtesy to all of this. As the Qur'an says: *"enter your houses by their [main] doors."*[9] We cannot be thieves coming through the

---

[9] Qur'an 2:189

windows. There is an order to things. If we are unclean outwardly, how can we talk about purification of the heart? If we are used to destructive ways of thinking, how can we have clear positive thoughts? We have to put our house in order from the outset. We have to begin where charity has to begin, which is with 'me', to put 'me' in order. Find out about our spectrum of totality, from one end of meanness to the other end of generosity. We must understand these things in ourselves.

Q: In your book [The Journey of the Self] you mention the purification of the heart quite extensively, and you have done so just now. Can you expound on how a person would go about to seek the purification of the heart and perhaps relate it to the teachings of Islam?

Within the Islamic traditions we have a fairly workable model for the human psyche as to what is soul, spirit, and what is mind or ''*aql*', heart or '*qalb*', and what is a whim. Basically we believe that the Islamic religion – and all other religions – are based on the same model, which is that the spirit is from beyond our comprehension, from the unknown and the unseen; it is from God. Once that spark interacts with matter, from it arises this ultimate complex thing called the self, the soul. So the soul is an individualistic thing, which we chisel and carve on in our lifetime as a result of interacting in the outer world through the mind and the intellect.

The heart remains the vehicle of interconnection or connection to the unknown, whereas the mind or the intellect is to do with duality, analysis and with causality, i.e. cause and effect. This is what that instrument or vehicle is for. The heart is to be 'empty', that is of anger, hatred, greed or envy. It is like a mirror, if it is tarnished it will not reflect reality. It is to be present, it is to be all available now, not tarnished by the past events or disturbed or concerned about the future events, therefore it is to do with beingness – pure simple beingness. The mind and the intellect have within them the network of experiences and relationships through the senses as we function in the outer physical world. The inner has its technology which is to be completely and utterly emptied out. Unless we are able to empty out, to learn the art of being inwardly clean, we are in '*shirk*' – in idolatry or polytheism.

The opposite of that situation is the '*nafs*', the ego and the arrogant self that wants to be acknowledged, to rule and wants to be totally dominating in this world. The secret of that is because there is a dominator of the entire creation beaming in our heart. Allah is in control of everything. If we connect to Him then in time He shapes our control. Allah is already in control and He is the *Al-Qahhar*, 'The Subduer' and *Al-Jabbar*, 'The Irresistible' or 'The Compeller'.

If we do not connect with Allah we may be perverted in simply feeding our ego and our lower self. We have to protect our inner condition so that it can be instantaneously purified, as the Qur'an describes: *"your enemy appear as your friend"* [10]. Somebody was your enemy one minute ago, suddenly the situation changes and now you love him and he loves you. Finished! You

---

[10] Qur'an 41:34

do not constantly remember three years ago, on the 2nd of August at four o'clock in the afternoon he was nasty to me, and I have written it in my diary and every day I look at it my heart is nothing other than poison.

Nobody with the right mind or condition wants to have the heart full of poison and puss. We all want to have good opinions of other people, we want to trust, love, and we want to be loved. We talked earlier of love for your neighbor, even if your neighbor is a person who is not of such a high desirable character but to have compassion for him or her and to know that he or she also has the possibility of evolving, and making their heart empty.

It does not mean that your mind is not recognizing that they are rascals or they are abusers in some form or another, or that they are ecologically not well behaved. You discriminate, but your heart is available immediately to turn towards love, compassion and toward magnanimity. Let us go back to the inner technology. The heart is to be empty and the mind full. Nowadays we often find the reverse, people's hearts are full of idols and their heads are empty.

After-Life in Islam

Q: In mentioning the soul and the development of the soul, it is obvious that you believe that the soul persists when the body is gone. In Islam is there belief in an after-life, in a reward for a correct and good life that is lived here on earth and the development of the soul during that life?

Like all other religions before it, in Islam the belief is that this existence in the physical domain is only a prelude to another phase. The same way as before this existence there was the phase of the womb. From the point of conception we are in a field of interspace. We are physically there but not aware of the physicality of the world. Then we are born into this world, which is like a kindergarten and here we have got limited possibilities of behavior. We can elevate ourselves, or we can devalue and lower ourselves. We have those choices. God has, in a sense, given us a certain amount of leeway. We can elevate ourselves to a point, according to the Qur'an, above the angels – the angelic powers and forces that are unknown and unseen by our senses – or we can sink to lower than brute animals. We encompass the entire spectrum, within ourselves, within this soul; it depends which one of them we are getting tuned to.

If you like it is like a radio. If we get ourselves constantly tuned to the higher, then we end up being the higher beings which we deserve to be. If, on the other hand, we choose lower then we are lower. During this life, it is like the university for us to practice this art of elevating ourselves according to our potential. After the release of the body, which belongs to the earth – it is only a borrowed vehicle – the soul carries on its journey to another interspace of the grave, until the world comes to an end. When physical creation comes to an end, we enter into a phase of non-time, non-space, so to speak; and this is the meaning of the hereafter or the after-life. We are, according to the Qur'an, allowed to have a pre-taste of that condition of leaving the body, and that is why the practices – the inner practices of Islam, the worship and the adoration and the meditation and all of the other

34

practices – are to focus us to that single-pointedness that will lead possibly to that awakening of gnosis, which is a taste of death, and which we recognize by it that death is nothing other than release of the soul. So it is an experiential situation, not something that is based on a dogma or a blind belief. We believe in that by that faith we will come to know it for certainty. We will have utter certainty that this is a short journey and that it is a takeoff point.

Islam & Science

Q: Shaykh Fadhlalla, you say that why the Universe was created lies beyond the grasp of Science. What is the Islamic viewpoint on the creation of the Universe?

Science is basically based on observation, and on fact-finding and on authenticating these facts by repetition and by experimentation. Science is a causal thing; it is to do with cause and effect. Creation, according to our faith, is, as Allah says to the Prophet Muhammad: *"I was a hidden treasure, and I loved to be known, and therefore I created."* The foundation of it all is based on love and it is to be known; so it is the Creator who loves to unveil himself to His creation. There cannot be a greater gift than that unveiling. The ultimate gift or purpose of creation is gnosis, to know that which is the only effulgent thing. It is not to know some 'thing' – that is necessary, that is science. The eye and the senses that are trained or we use in order to interrelate, to count and to measure are based and are functioning because of that

36

inner thing within them, the inner power within them; therefore, they will never be able to know the root or the essence of that power which is empowering them. Therefore science or technology will never have access to the root or the source of its emanation – where it came from.

Creation

Q: What you say is beautiful and it is very much in keeping with modern science. I was reading recently a book by Steven Hawking in which, of course, there is the theory of the "Big Bang" which originated about fifteen billion years ago in a sudden explosion. They can get to the very precise billionth of a billionth of a billionth of a second, but they do not know what was beyond that point; and even that theory of course has been questioned, as to whether there was really in a sense a beginning, or whether it always existed.

Well, going back to the earlier question you mentioned about the next life: we can have a taste of that by arrival at the point of total utter stillness. All attempts, in fact, every endeavor within mankind's efforts in this world, is to have that utter point of indescribable, inner, unfathomable silence, and that is the locus of the beginning of creation or the end of the creation, because it is the same. Either this way, or that way, it is time and space; it is a curve. So: we have access experientially not experimentally. Our mind and intellect, analyses and observations can only take us that far, beyond which we must take a jump without a parachute. That is called the art of submission, or that is where we really need faith, to simply 'be'. We have all been taught now to 'become' and that is science, but we have lost, in a way, in the recesses of our hearts how to be. It is sub-genetically imprinted in us to be, and that is where we take ourselves, to the point of the start of the visible movement of creation after the stillness.

Q: In Genesis, in the Bible, which you accept of course, it states that God says, "Let there be Light", and I know that has several meanings. Light, which is the beginning of all life in the Universe. But you mentioned earlier on, in our conversation, that something has no light. I know that word has a special meaning for you. Can you elaborate on the word Light?

By that I meant: 'no transmission', it is outer information.
It was actually referring to music. There is music, that is
fine, entertaining, and it sweeps you along. There is also
furniture music which is played in hotel lobbies; then
there is a sound, or a composition or a harmony that
awakens in us certain inner recesses that are almost at the
edge of time and space. They have a transformative
element. There are certain symphonies, other music,
certain creations and artistic work which have almost
taken that inspiration to the point beyond human
possibilities, and this is what we all strive for. We want
transformation. Information is only useful in existential
matters, but information, when it comes to matters of
awakening, gnosis or self-knowledge, is only useful if it is
going to transform us. Ultimately we are all seeking
ultimately transformation and that is what we want. When
there is 'no light', there is no transformation. Then it does
not ignite or enlighten that other part in us that we yearn
for it to be enlivened. It does not turn on that channel in
us, which we call the inner spiritual high, which is our

reality and the essence. And if we do not nourish that and nurture that happiness may elude us.

Light & Joy

Q: Should we then seek out experiences that will bring light to our lives and try to avoid, as much as possible, those that really put us in darkness?

No doubt! We naturally do that in our life though; observe how the child progresses. To begin with, a child is only concerned with causal events: the joy of seeing the laws of physics and gravity, and desires and how to satisfy desires, until we grow older. Then we begin to develop insight, wisdom develops, the windows to that inner light, until we begin to discover that real joy, ultimately, has its source within ourselves. Joy does not come from outside. It is we who create a certain need or desire and a gap from inside which we satisfy from the outside. This is only to bring about equilibrium out of a need: it is we who create that.

God Creates Light

Q: Can religion create light in our lives? And how does Islam create light?

It is Allah who creates light. God's purpose in creation is to ignite His creation, and to enliven His creation, each according to his potential: for the animal kingdom, according to the constraints that they live with; for human kind, to the ultimate, to know reality. But that knowledge is experiential, and that is the light. It is God's business. Religion is only to contain us, only to enable us to live within bounds that make this possibility more available for us. Prophets and Messengers only *indicate* God: it is we who have to collapse ourselves into our inner divine godliness by containment, by discrimination.

The religious path is only to enable us not to go for corruption and decadence and all that. Religion does not bring about godliness. God brings about His knowledge to whomever He wishes, as He wishes. The prophetically revealed knowledge is simply that there is one Reality.

That Reality encompasses all creation, but we have to awaken to it by abandoning to it, and then behaving ourselves by not getting corrupt or corrupting others and safeguarding our body, giving the body what it needs, not denying it, and not accepting that the body is all what there is.

Good & Evil

Q: Many people, religious and otherwise, often ask the question 'Why does God permit evil?' What would you reply to them?

There is a price to be paid for everything in our lives of consciousness. It is the rise and fall of Adam – and before that, creation. Before the rise of consciousness, there was none other than that placid, inanimate, or primal, total, ecological balance; there was no discrimination between opposites.

The rise of consciousness, the rise of conceptualization of a desire, with that wanting of the apple symbolizing this arose duality. Duality implies good and bad, healthy and unhealthy, it implies all of these opposites. Within us there is a discriminative quality: we do not want ill health; we do not like meanness; we do not like arrogance; we do not cherish hate.

There is, within us, that inner programming of orienting towards the higher virtues. We know what is going to destroy us. We are given that choice, in a way, to deal within these limitations. God has created this spectrum and has given us this discriminative capacity to work within that spectrum. In a sense, we have a choice, and yet we are programmed in essence to go towards that which elevates us towards that inner happiness, an inner state, which we all yearn for. God has given us a limited license. There is a limitation in that freedom, but we are free to choose.

Causes of Evil

Q: In the world we find many things that we consider to be evil, among them are hunger, crime, suffering, disease and poverty. What are your views of the cause and the function of evil in our lives?

Part of the philosophy is that we want to be happy. We do not want to be under the oppression of poverty, or of anxiety about today's supper. This is what God wants. Allah does not want us to be in misery and in desperation. That is why, we strive towards understanding, and how we can overcome these miseries.

But what happens is that we take this reality and conceptualize it into fear of poverty. Therefore, we hoard things, and are greedy, and excessive, until every one of us needs to have a garage sale once a month because we are kicking ourselves out of the house from over accumulation.

Nobody wants misery, stress or distress, but at the same time, we have a certain urge to interact with nature.

We have been given that facility of the intellect to interact with nature in order to learn this incredible, fantastic ecological equilibrium and inter-connectedness. So, we realize that we are part and parcel of a total physical reality, and yet we have emanated from a non-physical origin. We have a need, so to speak, which can easily be fulfilled, if we set about it in a manner that is conducive for the whole of humanity – not some part of humanity, at the expense of others, and ecologically disturb the world by displacement of resources from south to north and north to south. This is major upheaval: this is not what is meant. Therefore neither the north is happy, nor is the south happy. The whole of humanity is suffering from our excessive disturbance.

The Meaning of Suffering

Q: All of us in our lives will experience suffering at some time or other. We all face it. And you say that this could be considered to be a positive experience.

No doubt. Allah says in the Qur'an: *"[I have] written upon [myself] Mercy"[11]*. That means: mercy encompasses every situation and every experience.

I regard suffering as the barriers that will bring us back to the middle path or to the main road. If the barrier is not there we will go down to the valley, and end up totally destroyed. So, that suffering, that screeching, and that pain of not realizing our desires, is a reminder to us to ask: *who told us to have those desires, and is that a real desire, or is it a fancy one, or is it a real need*? We are all suffering to a great extent from our projections and from our conceptualizations, rather than the reality of the now. We suffer from an imaginary lack that we have put in ourselves and into our own minds or hearts. Suffering

---

[11] *"Say, 'To God. He has taken it upon Himself to be merciful."* – Qur'an 6:12

most of the time is illusionary and it is subjective, and therefore it is not real.

Q: How can we overcome that feeling of suffering, pain, anxiety and grief that we all go through?

By suffering. Nobody wants to suffer, so we learn to stop it, as we grow.

Overcoming Greed

Q: When you consider the ridiculousness of the situation, where you have people all wanting happiness, but they are fighting one another and pulling down someone else and robbing from someone, taking their land. This seems to be all against all religious principles, no matter what religion, and yet this type of acquisitiveness seems to persist in the world.

We have made our culture a culture of acquisition, a culture of progressive competition and aggression. Nowadays, if you describe somebody as being likely to succeed, you would say he is ambitious, competitive, aggressive and all that. We have been enhancing or trying to build up that aspect of our character that will bring about this doom, rather than cooperativeness, generosity, sharing and caring. And that is why we now have to re-balance that by bringing about a general care for our environment, for our neighbors, society and for humankind.

That is why I say there has to be a spiritual revival; otherwise, we are going to destroy ourselves, because we have taken it to such an extent that everyone of us has ended up as a totally separated individual: *me, and me, and me* – rather than realizing the 'me' is in *every* being, and therefore. taking what is necessary for me and enhancing the faith in me that the future will be all right if we collectively move towards that goal. But if we are all individuals, and if we are enhancing to simply care for our own personal individuality and fortune, then we will all end up in misfortune.

Compassion & Generosity

Q: The beautiful thought that you expressed earlier, that really has impressed itself upon me, is the Islamic idea that if there is any one person who is suffering in the world, then you cannot be happy as a Muslim. This is, I think, a very great thought that many people do not really associate with Islam.

Well, I am afraid it is because of the behavior of many Muslims; the same thing applies to the behavior of many so-called Christians. Where is there that there is no problem? It has become a *religion*, instead of a *way of life*, or of *beingness*, and therefore, to a certain extent, you will find some Muslims are barriers to the discovery of Islam by the rest of the world.

Not every '*Muslim*' is '*in Islam*': they are two separate things. Not *every* person who has an Islamic name is adhering to that faith and living it. A *Muslim* is somebody like myself who has inherited a name, a bit of reading and also accidentally knows (some) Arabic. It often causes

53

arrogance and assumptions which in themselves are the barriers.

Islam is the way of *beingness*: it is the way of *arrival*, the way of Allah and the way of '*Rasūlu'llah*', the prophet of God. It is not an ethnic Arab or a Middle Eastern preserve. It is a prophetically revealed knowledge that fits humankind, which has come at a time of ease of communication. It is easy to identify its authenticity because it is revealed in a language, which is still current, and we also know the conduct of the Prophet and those closest to him. But the majority of Muslims, or Muslim leaders do not adhere to it and therefore they are the barriers.

Q: How can Islam help us?

By constant reminders! The word for prayer is in Islam '*salāt*' and *salāt,* in the origin of the language, means 'to straighten a green twig or branch on a fire'. In a sense it is like an analogy of the human being. We all have a tendency to be crooked, not to be straight. But with faith and abandonment, we straighten. *Salāt* is to be plugged in to that condition, and to be willing to let go at any minute.

The Qur'an describes those who are in that state of awareness, that they are the ones who are perpetually in that natural state of awareness of reality. If you are in that state of awareness, then suffering is minimized. Suffering may still be on a physical level, which is a reminder that now I have stepped on a thorn and it is a deterrent – it is a healthy natural sign. If I do not have that sensation then I am very, very sick indeed.

Islamic Guidelines & Practices

Q: I observed, in my limited experience with some Muslims, that it is their practice, never to question the motives of Allah or God. Is this a fact?

Muslims are inspired by the prophetic teaching never to discuss Allah, that which can never be known in its entirety. Instead, they are to discuss the *attributes* of God and God's creation, to wonder about nature and learn about everything.

How can we talk about Allah who already encompasses everything? How can you question that which itself brings about the source of questioning? However, we must question: *What are we doing? Why are we doing it?* We must question our intentions and the results of our actions. We must question our interactions with nature, with each other, and with oneself. All of this is subject to question, but Allah, who has created the possibility and the energy that causes that question, is beyond questioning. Many Muslims seem to mix up things because their intellect, scientific knowledge, causality, or rationality is not sufficiently developed: we say it is to do with Allah. It is not so.

Trust in Allah

Q: I always find that when a Muslim says 'Allah', it is with great love and respect, whereas I have an interest in studying religions, and I notice that in some other religions people will say 'God, why did you impose that burden upon me? Why must I suffer this?' questioning the motives. And that has inspired a great respect in me for Islam.

Basically it has to do with faith, and that whatever has happened has its reasons, some understandable, some not, but because of the fact that it has happened, a Muslim resolves that it must be real *because it has happened*. Half of it may be because of my ignorance and the other half because I was not aware of what was going on in it the sense of cause and effect.

Accepting what has happened in good faith will enable me and give me an advantage to understand what was the actual reason for its happening or that it was unavoidable: *I was aware, I did my best, and yet that was it.* For every experience there are reasons, not all these reasons are fully understandable. In my own experience, I have often found that things I was aiming for were not realized, and there may be a momentary disappointment, but if I waited a bit I found that it was for my own good and in retrospect I am so grateful that what I aimed for did not happen. God is the most generous and has mercy upon all situations, but it is my ignorance of the situation and my own state, with regard to that situation, that causes this so-called friction or disappointment. We have faith in that whatever has happened, if we are worthy of understanding it, then we know it is to our benefit. We turn whatever negative situation into potential growth and positiveness.

Salāt **or Prayers**

Q: That leads me to ask another question, and that is the practice of praying. Muslims pray five times a day. What is the nature of the prayers of Muslims?

Basically, again, we start from the point of duality and the point of physical separateness that we are in and by pointing to a symbolic center, which is the house of God, towards which we face in our prayers.

There is no place that God does not dwell in, but this is the symbolic place where the prophet Abraham built in order for people to point towards or come to and adore their Lord in a space where there is no outer distraction, almost in the middle of a desert, with hardly any vegetation or any other growth. So you would go there only for the purpose of practicing beingness. The start of '*salāt*', or prayers, is to point towards that symbolic pure house of God and after that there is a dialogue between you and God.

By standing up you praise that reality and after that you are struck by its magnificence; you bend and prostrate and you go down to obliterate all your senses, in a way, and abandon into it. The most precious faculties you have are in the face, so you completely obliterate that profile into its nothingness, and therefore into your beingness, so to speak.

Then you again sit up from that prostration to observe duality, to know that there is also the so-called 'I'. It is a practice of diving into the inner, unfathomable, non-experienceable dimension, and yet acknowledging the fact that you and the soul still exist. All of this happens when you have abandoned the mind and thoughts.

And as part of offering your prayer you do ablution: the ritualistic cleansing that takes place before prayer. It is not to do with cleaning – we are supposed to be clean anyway – but it is to seal the senses and the limbs so you are now sealed from outside interferences, and you are focused entirely into that state.

That is the meaning of *salāt*!

Islamic Rituals and the Hajj

Q: That is the most beautiful and clearest definition I have had of the prayer of the Muslim. It is very, very beautiful.

Let me ask you another question: what is the nature of Hajj?

All Islamic rituals – as a matter of fact, all religious rituals – have inner meanings. There are outer practices, but they all have inner meanings as well and these inner meanings are all available. The heart is supposed to be our sanctum: our '*Ka`bah*'.

When we go for '*hajj*', the pilgrimage, the '*ka`bah*' is supposed to be empty with no idols in it, and no inner secrets, desires or attachments. Similarly our heart is supposed to be empty as well.

One of our greatest masters, Imam Ali, says: *"To renounce the world does not mean not to own anything, it means that nothing should own you"*. We cannot renounce matter – our physical body is made of matter –

but it depends on our interrelationship with it: does my car own me, do I own the car? If the car is scratched, am I scratched, or is it yet another acquisition, a necessary acquisition? There is a problem, but it is surmountable.

The Purpose of Prayer

Q: Just to keep on the topic of prayer: does a Muslim ever pray to Allah for something, to receive something? What you have mentioned is the praise of Allah and also a realization of yourself in the wonder of God, but does a Muslim ever pray for some material goods?

Since Allah contains all realities, physical, non-physical, observable, non-observable, and since we encompass the physical all the way down to the inner sublime, and since we are all programmed wanting equilibrium at all levels, we want physical equilibrium, we want to be physically nurtured and satisfied, we also want our mind to be in the right state.

So we call upon that Reality throughout this demand or spectrum of needs. We supplicate and constantly call upon that Reality to show us how we can improve our health, physical situation, and the purification of our hearts. At all times we are actually calling upon Allah to guide us to that beingness.

Sometimes it will be through means – a person, an environment, a teacher, and a generous person – but we always envision that the manifestation of the answer has emanated from the unseen into the seen. So therefore we thank Allah all the time and also we thank the creation, which has helped us to that.

The Prophet says that if you do not thank creation, you would not have thanked Allah. The Prophet (also) says that creation is the family of God, and those of you who are most useful to creation is most loved by God. It is an evolving movement; it is a process of arrival.

Answers to Prayers

Q: So you do pray to Allah for guidance, for certain help, for certain things that you desire. I have heard it said that, and I know from my own experience, people who have prayed for a sick child – someone who was dying – and yet the person died, and the parents were very disappointed, and they would say: "Why has God taken that child from me? My prayers were not answered". What would you say to such a parent?

The answer is actually based on what we perceive as the *answer* to the prayer. It may be much better for the child to leave now than, say, in a year's time, when he or she might have been in a far more complex situation, or ending up having a child for twenty years who is having to be sustained by all kinds of devices. We do not necessarily understand God's mercy at all times. My business is to expect the best, ask for the best, and do my best for the best. The exact specific outcome may not be what I had envisioned.

As I was saying earlier, we conceptualize. We can ask God to give us the best possibility, the best condition of the heart, the best equilibrium or the best possible health. But if I have genetically inherited certain deficiencies that may be the base from which I will start. God creates according to laws; it is not chaos, it is cosmos. We should not simply expect God to stop the rain when there may be another thousand people praying for rain.

We do not know God's ways; we have to be sincere to our own ways, making that request with sincerity, with the purest intention, and doing our best for it. But the results are not in our hands.

We do not know what is the nature of the next life. That is ultimately where everything will end up anyway. We can only seek the best possible outcome in the sense of not being encumbered more than we are in the physical body.

We say our prayers for the child, the neighbor, humanity, but if the majority of humanity decides to continue doing what it does we will end up being in the wilderness as the prophet Moses was for forty odd years.

He and his people could not enter Jerusalem, even though he was a prophet of God, and that is how it is. So many other prophets amongst their own people went along with the situation, knowing that it could not change because of the nature of the people. There are laws and you cannot transgress them.

Having Faith in God

Q: In other words you are saying that a person should never be discouraged by the results, no matter how bad the results happen to be in a particular situation.

Absolutely!

The situation may appear to be bad at that moment, but if we are sincere and our hearts are pure we will soon know that what happened is for the best. Allah says in the Qur'an: *"With every difficulty there is an ease. With the difficulty there is an ease."*[12] It implies that with every one difficulty there are two eases. One ease is that the difficulty will pass whatever it may be, it will pass, and at the end we will die anyway. Then He says that with *the* difficulty there is also ease, if we understand the ecological perfection of that occurrence. That understanding also brings about ease. That is why we want to know: how did I become ill? Why did I have that infection? And the answer will be either weakness,

---

[12] Qur'an 94:5-6

vitamin deficiency, over-exposure or increased stress. By that so-called analytical understanding we are a bit eased, although the illness is still there.

The more we have an open heart, the more we will know what is happening is perfect, according to a balance, and we can not go back in time, we can only go forward. As you say there is no discouragement. Allah says in the Qur'an: *"Never ever feel sorry for that which has passed, and never look with expectations about the future."*[13] Have faith and a good opinion, have a positive outlook, but do not conceptualize exactly how the future will turn out.

You may say: "At thirty-five I will have this house and that car." But by that time, you may have an ulcer, or the job has fallen through. There is no way you can know these events exactly. The way of beingness is in the *now*, in the *present*, when all the energies are available; therefore, even the physical outcome is likely to be the

---

[13] Based on, *"so that you may not grieve for what you missed or for what happened to you."* – Qur'an 3:153

best it can be. It is as simple as that. It is the only positive outlook that a human being can have, and that is why we have no choice in that. Talking about the freedom of no choice is this: we have no choice but to be in that positive state and be most efficient at it.

Social Responsibilities

Q: The Qur'an talks about man's outer code of social responsibility and his path of inner purification. Would you give us the views of the Islamic faith on the social responsibility that we have?

In our modern culture, in the West, we have the fields of psychology, sociology, and all the other so called sciences.

In the field of spiritual sciences we have similar sorts of divisions, the individual and societal, and the individual reflects the societal prism. In other words, our first responsibility is towards the discovery of our own self, and we have repeated teachings and indications that *"He who knows himself knows his Lord"*. It is through the knowledge of the self that we recognize this incredible reflection of other realities, because we believe in the microcosm reflecting the macrocosm. Whatever exists outside that I can appreciate or understand and comprehend, must have its origin within me; otherwise, I cannot reflect it, or understand it. So my first responsibility is towards my self. *Who am I? Why am I here? What is the meaning of death? Why am I heading towards this recycling of the body after gaining all these experiences and wisdom, and having consumed so much of this world and caused so much havoc in it? What is the meaning of it? Where is the justice in it?*

If we understand the self, then a new process of compassion and understanding and magnanimity will occur for the rest of humanity. Allah says in the Qur'an: *"[I] created you from one self and from it its pairs"[14]*.

We are essentially one self: every one of us wants the same thing. We want harmony, we want love, we want attention, we want good relationships, and we do not want the unknown.

If my responsibility towards my self – which is towards Godliness within me – is fulfilled, then it is likely my responsibility towards the rest of creation is lighter. Society is only a multiplicity of me. So in order to know

---

[14] Qur'an 4:1

'me', in order to empty out, or to take that ultimate pilgrimage, an individual must be able to do it by himself or herself. It is the pilgrimage to Makkah: to go with passion and love, give up, give in, with total and utter faith – it is a passion.

Having discovered that this so called 'me' is only an outer shadow of that inner reality that has no time and space, one is equipped to come back to this world and serve. It is then that we need the societal code of conduct. It is then that we need the laws, the natural laws that were revealed to prophets: to be generous, compassionate and to interact correctly, not to be too greedy, not to interact in a usurious fashion, and so on and so forth.

In a way, to exaggerate, to know God, you do not need anything except giving up everything, but to know humankind and society you need to know a prophet, you need to adhere to prophetic codes of conduct, otherwise, society will be damaged and ruined, and only be fit for recycling.

Faith, Love & Action

Q: The Islamic view is that action is a part of faith, a very important part. God is not merely concerned with a person's beliefs – valuable though they may be – but also with his or her doings, especially as they affect other people. Could you comment upon that?

According to the Qur'an, Allah says: *"Allah will hold you questioned, or you will reap the rewards of what is in your heart"*. What is ultimately within the recesses of your heart, you will see and experience in the world and the hereafter.

It implies that your intentions, which also emanate in outer actions, are really what you are making of yourself. Because reality encompasses the seen and the unseen, you cannot separate action from intention. In other words, your actions, in the long run, are going to indicate your intentions. If your intentions are genuine, sincere and honorable, eventually your actions will also be regarded, accepted or experienced as such. Actions are the realization of intentions. If your intention is to share and care with love and understanding, even though it may at first be misunderstood, or the person to whom you want to give that love is too ill to receive it, or perhaps will not accept it, that love will still prevail.

Actions are the outer manifestations of intentions: you are, therefore, in this life actually building your soul. You are chiseling your soul by your intentions and actions – you cannot separate them. There is a unitive reality that encompasses it. You cannot have intentions of love and generosity and yet constantly be causing havoc, damage and greed: it cannot be.

Now, we cannot question each other on intentions though, but we can question each other on actions. According to Islamic law, or outer judgment, we can only be judged according to the results of what we have done outwardly. We cannot be questioned on what is in our hearts: that is a matter between you and God.

However, God's mercy is such that, as I said, ultimately actions and intentions do show – they are connected anyway.

To get back to your question, does it answer it?

Q: Yes, it does. One of the reasons for asking it is that, in some religions, take the Christian religion, some Christians say that faith alone is sufficient for salvation. I personally believe that works are more important, and this seems to be the Islamic philosophy, too?

You know when they say faith alone is sufficient, I understand by that: if faith is the primary factor, that is what we put all our investment in, if we have that total trust, then faith alone will eventually also end up being the actions we undertake, and which will be right.

Faith alone does not mean cutting up faith from the other realities that are connected with faith. If I have complete and utter faith in the mercy of Reality and its total love, then definitely faith alone is enough because eventually, it will prevail. But if faith is cut off from its outer visibility, then it is not faith, it is a phantom.

Justice

Q: Correct me if I am wrong, but I believe that in your book [The Journey of the Self] you say one of the greatest virtues is justice. Do you believe that to be so, and why so?

Justice in the original sense of it, as the Qur'an says or as the prophetic way was, is based on an Arabic term ''*adl*'. ''*Adl*' means to be in the middle, the medium, the middle of the road, the path of maximum balance and maximum vision. And this is what we constantly want, whether we are driving on the road, or in any circumstance, we want to be in the safest lane, not on the extreme of either deprivation or excess, or immense poverty or superfluous wealth.

The seed of justice is in every heart, in fact. And that is what causes us to talk about conscience, or what gives us bad conscience, or guilt. There is something within us that somehow guides us, that says: "this is unfair", "this is out of balance", and therefore we will all be in imbalance if we adhere to that edge.

Justice is an essential concept in that it is the ultimate and the main attribute of God. God is Just! God is just in this world, but we can apparently interfere in that justice as human beings. But in the hereafter, there is total justice, in that we will only experience and be rewarded according to what we have made of our lives.

Here it appears as though there is injustice. God says in the Qur'an: *"Do not mistake human injustices as God's punishment"* [15]. It is human injustice, and if we are intelligent enough we translate that circumstance of being subjective to injustice to inner purification, or inner understanding, or whatever. So we can use every circumstance to which we are subjected to betterment: it can be inner betterment; it can be patience, to learn how

---

[15] Full verse: *"There are some people who say, 'We believe in God,' but, when they suffer for His cause, they think that human persecution is as severe as God's punishment yet, if any help comes to you [Prophet] from your Lord, they will say, 'We have always been with you'. Does God not know best what is in everyone's hearts?"* – Qur'an 29:10

to be patient with that circumstance, or abusive environment, or abusive and unjust treatment, or whatever.

A Code of Justice

Q: Does the Islamic religion have a code of justice? Does it provide some general guidance, or are there some specific codes of justice that the Muslims must adhere to?

There are general umbrella-like guidances, which are acceptable to Reality, i.e. that these are the natural ways. Within them then those who are most spiritually evolved are supposed to bring about transitory or temporary laws or measures.

If society is ruled by the philosopher king, or the most spiritually evolved being, then that being has to adhere to the Qur'an and to the prophetic way, which is a broad umbrella, such as, for example, not to own excess or extra provisions when there are people close to you who are not able to fulfill their immediate needs.

Equally, for example, on land-ownership: it tells us you are allowed to use whatever land or whatever resources your needs justify. Now those needs must be real, not fantasies. The philosophical root of this is that no Muslim is supposed to own a lot of land lying fallow for year after year. The spiritual leader of that community should take him to task and revert that land back to those who need it; but if the fellow is going to need the land next year or the year after, he is given time. It must be based on justice; otherwise, where is the justice in the feudal lordship that we see now in so many Muslim countries, where people owning thousands of acres are not able to cultivate the land, and not even intending to cultivate it when others do not have anything?

You therefore find these Muslim governments having to invent their own laws of land reform, or socialism, or whatever. By doing so, they will bring about another form of oppression, rather than more benign self-regulating rules that enable society to grow more organically forward hand in hand, with everybody questioning each other's situation in a natural way.

Justice permeates all the way down to the day-to-day life. For example, as you know, a Muslim is prohibited from drinking alcohol because it is an intoxicant and has side-effects; yet, if the so-called Muslim drinks in a quiet, subdued, secret way, you and I are not allowed to interfere according to the spiritual leader: he will not accept our evidence if we had spied upon that person. It does not allow us to spy upon another person who is intoxicating himself alone, because he is at least not causing damage to society, or in a sense enticing others towards things that, in the long run, can be abusive and could cause troubles.

So there are these broad umbrella-like rules and laws, but within them there are leeways. Circumstantial situations may cause the ongoing leadership to make certain modifications within them; you cannot go beyond them. You cannot make usury acceptable: according to Islam, you cannot accept usury, no matter how.

Restriction & Freedom

Q: There are some non-Muslims who consider Islam to be somewhat restrictive, but the Qur'an indicates that the individual is given the freedom, a great deal of freedom, particularly to follow the path of wholesomeness. Can you tell us what that path of wholesomeness would imply?

The 'path of wholesomeness' implies outer restrictions: there are outer limitations. For example, physically we are limited. In fact, we peak in our physical performance during our thirties and forties and then we begin to decline. It is a natural restriction as to how much time or life we have, or in how many places we can sleep, or how much we can eat.

So there are natural limitations.

Inwardly, there is no limitation to our state. The path of wholesomeness is to recognize natural outer restrictions and accept them because they are the natural laws. If you are abusive in the long run you will also be abused. If you are greedy you become a model of greed, then that society or that community you live in is going to go on a rampage, and so on.

So wholesomeness consists of the outer restrictions, bounds and courtesies. Inwardly, we can be unrestricted, depending on the extent of our inner freedom, inner non-attachment and the condition of our hearts.

The Christian Trinity

Q: Muslims accept Jesus as a great prophet, but not as the Son of God. Can you tell us why Muslims do not accept Jesus as the Son of God?

According to the Qur'an and the prophetic teachings, God is that Reality which transcends all other realities and all other existences, and there is nothing like Him. From that definition we can say that everything emanates from God, is caused by God, but it is not the situation of father and son relationship.

In a sense God is the 'father' of all creation, but He is not a father in the existential sense of fatherliness: He is the source from which everything has emanated. And Jesus is a prophet, he is a being who reflected total godliness and total God-knowledge, and he was the most unusual of all prophets in that he came from an immaculate conception – and incidentally, there are more references about Jesus in the Qur'an than about Muhammad. He is a reflector of God, and he is a true manifestation of divine possibility within the human frame.

The Prophets of Islam

Q: There are many Christians who do not really know that the Muslims hold Jesus in such high esteem, and refer to him with such great respect. This is unfortunate. There are many who do not know that the Muslims accept certain books from the Bible, as being the revealed word of God. In the matter of the teachings of Jesus, are most Muslims aware of some of the sayings and teachings of Jesus?

There is a large body of traditions that is acceptable truth within Islam: one of them is the teaching of Jesus.

However, there are some on which doubt has been cast.

For example, we consider Jesus to be infallible; we consider all prophets to be infallible. We cannot accept prophets who have exercised certain behavior that is far from being normally accepted as part of the human behavior. We consider these as either misrepresentations or freaks that have occurred in those traditions. We hold Jesus, Moses and all the other prophets in the highest esteem, but most of all, of course, Moses and Jesus, because Islam is a continuation of that culture, or that part of the world civilization. As a result, great deals of the Judaic teachings are totally acceptable within the Islamic teaching.

Islam – A Choice Today

Q: Does Islam provide solutions to world problems today, and if so, why are Muslims suffering and struggling more than people of other nations and religions?

Allah has not created this existence for us to suffer. Suffering is that which is to be avoided in this existence. So it is natural for us to want to avoid suffering on a personal scale, on a collective scale, and on a humankind scale. If we are suffering, it means that we have transgressed natural laws. It is not intended for us collectively to behave as we do. How this suffering has come about is something that can be analyzed easily historically and seen as cause and effect. We may still want to keep on, because we say we are not willing to give up whatever it is that we have to give up, in order to stop, redress, counterbalance and antidote for the poisonous situations we have brought upon ourselves.

Islam provides us the faith of beingness and unfoldment within ourselves in the sense that it also provides for us the bounds that we are taught by the prophetic knowledge not to transgress, that if we keep within these bounds the suffering will be minimum and it will only be as an aspect of teaching; otherwise, it can be catastrophic.

Allah has created this entire creation out of love and for Him to be known. And that requires a certain commitment and adherence from humankind. If we maintain that loyalty and sincerity, then the suffering will be at a minimum, and it will be suffering in order to appreciate joy, in order to appreciate its opposite, not a prevalent suffering under which we are all being weighted.

The behavior of Muslims is a reflection of that. If they are within laws and bounds, if their hearts are empty and pure and they genuinely apply the outer practices and rituals with the inner meanings, then there will be no suffering, and there will be prevalence of that knowledge, because it is *transmittive*. But if they do not, and they only give lip service to it, or they render it into a ritualistic procedure without a heart, without a meaning, then of course again it reflects the state they are in.

Personal Choice of Religion

Q: Another question is that of a religion being a matter of personal choice. Is it a matter of personal choice, or is it something that most people adopt because of their ethnic origin, perhaps their cultural pressures or even their upbringing?

Well, a way to Reality – which religion is – is a way to discovery and awakening. It is a bit like inheritance: we all want wealth, but inherited wealth is often not appreciated and often is abused or taken for granted. Many of us who were brought up in an Islamic environment take it for granted. Yet we may have deviated considerably from the inner reality of it because again we have assumed, so then the cultural inheritance becomes a barrier and an aberration.

Awakening, inner fulfillment and inner purity are definitively a personal exercise based on a choice. You cannot impose Islam upon anyone, even though they may have inherited it. In fact, Muslims in societies or in environments that are healthy, like Canada, who rediscover their heritage, are far more real in their Islam than an average person in a culturally Islamic environment. There are always exceptions anyway. Rediscovery depends very much upon the individual, the home environment, the cultural environment, and the social environment.

eBooks By Zahra Publications

General eBooks on Islam

Living Islam – East and West

Shaykh Fadhlalla Haeri

Ageless and universal wisdom set against the backdrop of a changing world: application of this knowledge to one's own life is most appropriate.

The Elements of Islam

Shaykh Fadhlalla Haeri

An introduction to Islam through an overview of the universality and light of the prophetic message.

The Qur'an & Its Teachings

Journey of the Universe as Expounded in the Qur'an

Shaykh Fadhlalla Haeri

The Qur'an traces the journey of all creation, seeing the physical, biological and geological voyage of life as paralleled by the inner spiritual evolution of woman/man.

Keys to the Qur'an: Volume 1: Commentary on Surah Al-Fatiha and Surah Al-Baqarah

Shaykh Fadhlalla Haeri

95

The first two chapters of the Qur'an give guidance regarding inner and outer struggle. Emphasis is on understanding key Qur'anic terms.

Keys to the Qur'an: Volume 2: Commentary on Surah Ale-`Imran

Shaykh Fadhlalla Haeri

A commentary on the third chapter of the Qur'an, the family of `Imran which includes the story of Mary, mother of `Isa (Jesus).

Keys to the Qur'an: Volume 3: Commentary on Surah Yasin

Shaykh Fadhlalla Haeri

Commentary on chapter *Yasin*. This is traditionally read over the dead person: if we want to know the meaning of life, we have to learn about death.

Keys to the Qur'an: Volume 4: Commentary on Surahs Al-`Ankabut, Al-Rahman, Al-Waqi`ah and Al-Mulk

Shaykh Fadhlalla Haeri

The Shaykh uncovers inner meanings, roots and subtleties of the Qur'anic Arabic terminology in these four selected Surahs.

Keys to the Qur'an: Volume 5: Commentary on Juz' `Amma

Shaykh Fadhlalla Haeri

Insight into the last *Juz'* of Qur'an, with the objective of exploring the deeper meanings of Qur'anic Revelations.

The Essential Message of the Qur'an

eBooks By Zahra Publications

Shaykh Fadhlalla Haeri

Teachings from the Qur'an such as purpose of creation, Attributes of the Creator, nature of human beings, decrees governing the laws of the universe, life and death.

The Qur'an in Islam: Its Impact & Influence on the Life of Muslims

`Allamah Sayyid M. H. Tabataba`i

`Allamah Sayyid M. H. Tabataba`i shows in this gem how the Qur'an contains the fundamental roots of Islam and the proof of prophethood as the Word of God.

The Qur'anic Prescription for Life

Shaykh Fadhlalla Haeri

Understanding the Qur'an is made accessible with easy reference to key issues concerning life and the path of Islam.

The Story of Creation in the Qur'an

Shaykh Fadhlalla Haeri

An exposition of the Qur'anic verses relating to the nature of physical phenomena, including the origins of the universe, the nature of light, matter, space and time, and the evolution of biological and sentient beings.

Sufism & Islamic Psychology and Philosophy

Beginning's End

Shaykh Fadhlalla Haeri

This is a contemporary outlook on Sufi sciences of self knowledge, exposing the challenge of our modern lifestyle that is out of balance.

Cosmology of the Self

Shaykh Fadhlalla Haeri

Islamic teachings of *Tawhīd* (Unity) with insights into the human self: understanding the inner landscape is essential foundation for progress on the path of knowledge.

Decree and Destiny (Original and a Revised Version)

Shaykh Fadhlalla Haeri

A lucid exposition of the extensive body of Islamic thought on the issue of free will and determinism.

Happiness in Life and After Death – An Islamic Sufi View

Shaykh Fadhlalla Haeri

This book offers revelations and spiritual teachings that map a basic path towards wholesome living without forgetting death: cultivating a constant awareness of one's dual nature.

Leaves from a Sufi Journal

Shaykh Fadhlalla Haeri

A unique collection of articles presenting an outstanding introduction to the areas of Sufism and original Islamic teachings.

The Elements of Sufism

Shaykh Fadhlalla Haeri

Sufism is the heart of Islam. This introduction describes its origins, practices, historical background and its spread throughout the world.

The Garden of Meaning

Shaykh Fadhlalla Haeri

This book is about two gardens, one visible and fragrant, the other less visible but eternal. The beauty and harmony of both gardens are exposited in this magisterial volume, linking outer to inner, physics to metaphysics, self to cosmos.

The Journey of the Self

Shaykh Fadhlalla Haeri

After introducing the basic model of the self, there follows a simple yet complete outline of the self's emergence, development, sustenance, and growth toward its highest potential.

The Sufi Way to Self-Unfoldment

Shaykh Fadhlalla Haeri

Unfolding inner meanings of the Islamic ritual practices towards the intended ultimate purpose to live a fearless and honorable life, with no darkness, ignorance or abuse.

Witnessing Perfection

Shaykh Fadhlalla Haeri

Delves into the universal question of Deity and the purpose of life. Durable contentment is a result of 'perfected vision'.

Practices & Teachings of Islam

Calling Allah by His Most Beautiful Names
Shaykh Fadhlalla Haeri

Attributes or Qualities resonate from their Majestic and Beautiful Higher Realm into the heart of the active seeker, and through it back into the world.

Fasting in Islam
Shaykh Fadhlalla Haeri

This is a comprehensive guide to fasting in all its aspects, with a description of fasting in different faith traditions, its spiritual benefits, rules and regulations.

Prophetic Traditions in Islam: On the Authority of the Family of the Prophet
Shaykh Fadhlalla Haeri

Offers a comprehensive selection of Islamic teachings arranged according to topics dealing with belief and worship, moral, social and spiritual values.

The Wisdom (Hikam) of Ibn `Ata'allah: Translation and Commentary
Translation & Commentary by Shaykh Fadhlalla Haeri

These aphorisms of Ibn `Ata'Allah, a Shadhili Shaykh, reveal the breadth and depth of an enlightened being who reflects divine unity and inner transformation through worship.

The Inner Meanings of Worship in Islam: A Personal Selection of Guidance for the Wayfarer

Shaykh Fadhlalla Haeri

Guidance for those who journey along this path, from the Qur'an, the Prophet's traditions, narrations from the *Ahl al-Bayt*, and seminal works from among the *Ahl al-Tasawwuf* of all schools of thought.

The Lantern of The Path

Imam Ja`far Al-Sadiq

Each one of the ninety-nine chapter of this book is a threshold to the next, guiding the reader through the broad spectrum of ageless wisdom, like a lantern along the path of reality.

The Pilgrimage of Islam

Shaykh Fadhlalla Haeri

This is a specialized book on spiritual journeying, offering the sincere seeker keys to inner transformation.

The Sayings & Wisdom of Imam `Ali

Compiled By: Shaykh Fadhlalla Haeri
Translated By: Asadullah ad-Dhaakir Yate

Carefully translated into modern English, a selection of this great man's sayings gathered together from authentic and reliable sources.

Transformative Worship in Islam: Experiencing Perfection

Shaykh Fadhlalla Haeri with Muna H. Bilgrami

This book uniquely bridges the traditional practices and beliefs, culture and language of Islam with the transformative spiritual states described by the Sufis and Gnostics.

Talks, Interviews & Courses

Ask Course ONE: The Sufi Map of the Self

Shaykh Fadhlalla Haeri

This workbook explores the entire cosmology of the self through time, and maps the evolution of the self from before birth through life, death and beyond.

Ask Course TWO: The Prophetic Way of Life

Shaykh Fadhlalla Haeri

This workbook explores how the code of ethics that govern religious practice and the Prophetic ways are in fact transformational tools to enlightened awakening.

Friday Discourses: Volume 1

Shaykh Fadhlalla Haeri

The Shaykh addresses many topics that influence Muslims at the core of what it means to be a Muslim in today's global village.

Songs of Iman on the Roads of Pakistan

Shaykh Fadhlalla Haeri

A series of talks given on the divergence between 'faith' and 'unbelief ' during a tour of the country in 1982 which becomes a reflection of the condition occurring in the rest of the world today.

The Connection Between the Absolute and the Relative

Shaykh Fadhlalla Haeri

This is a 1990 conversation with Shaykh Fadhlalla Haeri, in which he talks about wide-ranging topics on Islam and presents it as the archetypal, universal, Adamic path that began when humanity rose in consciousness to recognize duality and began its journey from the relative back to Absolute Unity.

The Spiritual Path: A Conversation with Shaykh Fadhlalla Haeri On His Life, Thought and Work

Professor Ali A. Allawi

In this wide-ranging conversation with Professor Ali Allawi, Shaykh Fadhlalla Haeri talks about his life story and the spiritual journey that he embarked on and the path he has been on ever since.

Poetry, Aphorisms & Inspirational

101 Helpful Illusions

Shaykh Fadhlalla Haeri

Everything in creation has a purpose relevant to ultimate spiritual Truth. This book highlights natural veils to be transcended by disciplined courage, wisdom and insight.

Beyond Windows

Shaykh Fadhlalla Haeri

Offering moving and profound insights of compassion and spirituality through these anthologies of connections between slave self and Eternal Lord.

Bursts of Silence

Shaykh Fadhlalla Haeri

Inspired aphorisms provide keys to doors of inner knowledge, as well as antidotes to distraction and confusion.

Pointers to Presence

Shaykh Fadhlalla Haeri

A collection of aphorisms providing insights into consciousness and are pointers to spiritual awakening.

Ripples of Light

Shaykh Fadhlalla Haeri

Inspired aphorisms which become remedies for hearts that seek the truth.

Sound Waves

Shaykh Fadhlalla Haeri

A collection of aphorisms that help us reflect and discover the intricate connection between self and soul.

Sublime Gems: Selected Teachings of Shaykh Abd al-Qadir al-Jilani

Shaykh Abd al-Qadir al-Jilani

Spiritual nourishment extracted from Shaykh Abd al-Qadir al-Jilani's existing works.

Autobiography

Son of Karbala

Shaykh Fadhlalla Haeri

The atmosphere of an Iraq in transition is brought to life and used as a backdrop for the Shaykh's own personal quest for self-discovery and spiritual truth.

Health Sciences and Islamic History

Health Sciences in Early Islam – Volumes 1 & 2

Collected Papers By: Sami K. Hamarneh
Edited By: Munawar A. Anees
Foreword By: Shaykh Fadhlalla Haeri

Health Sciences in Early Islam is a pioneering study of Islamic medicine that opens up new chapters of knowledge in the history of the healing sciences. This two volume work covers the development of Islamic medicine between the 6th and 12th centuries A.D.

www.ingramcontent.com/pod-product-compliance
Lightning Source LLC
LaVergne TN
LVHW011400080426
835511LV00005B/360